Original title:
Eclipses and Epics

Copyright © 2025 Creative Arts Management OÜ
All rights reserved.

Author: Hugo Fitzgerald
ISBN HARDBACK: 978-1-80567-828-1
ISBN PAPERBACK: 978-1-80567-949-3

Legends Lost in Shadow

In the sky a big ol' slice,
The moon thinks it's a big device.
Blocking sunlight with a grin,
A game of peek-a-boo to win.

Knights in armor lost their way,
Chasing shadows gone astray.
They tripped on capes, fell in mud,
And blamed it all on cosmic thud.

A dragon snoozed beneath the haze,
Dreaming of his glory days.
When he awoke, he let out a roar,
Only to find he'd missed the score.

A wizard muttered charms unfurled,
But his spells just swirled and twirled.
He turned a prince into a frog,
And forgot the secret of the fog.

Portents of the Darkened Horizon

A shadow dances on the moon,
A raccoon tries to sing a tune.
With snacks galore in hand, we rush,
To see the day turn night in a hush.

People stare with eyes so wide,
As the cheese wheel rolls down the slide.
A hungry bear in a space suit,
Complains that there's no food to loot.

Sagas Written in Starlight

In the silence, stars have tales,
Of tiny fish who ride on whales.
They surf the waves of cosmic cream,
And tell us life is but a dream.

An owl wears glasses, reads the night,
And says, "You're all a funny sight!"
With every wink, the skies reply,
As laughter echoes from on high.

A Symphony of Cosmic Whispers

The planets hum a silly song,
As comets dance, they twirl along.
A tuba's blare from Mars so bright,
Makes Saturn giggle with delight.

While meteors throw glittery sprinkles,
Stars brag about their shining twinkles.
Jupiter's moons join in the spree,
Singing loudly, "Look at me!"

The Shrouded Ascent

Climbing up in robes so grand,
A sunbeam zaps, oh isn't it planned?
With clouds as pillows, soft and light,
Dreamers wrestle with pure delight.

The party's up where no one sees,
As laughter hangs upon the breeze.
A cat in space has lost its way,
It swirls around, still wants to play.

The Lurking Light

In shadows cast, the moon plays hide,
While sunbeams laugh and dance worldwide.
A cosmic game of peek-a-boo,
The stars roll their eyes, oh what a view!

The roaches cheer, they love this show,
As beams of light put on a glow.
The sun yells, "Hey, I'm still right here!"
But the moon just smirks, it's time for beer!

Fables of the Silent Cosmos

Once in the sky, a tale was spun,
The planets giggled, oh what fun!
Comets raced with tails like cats,
While aliens brewed interstellar chats.

Giant dust bunnies, twinkling bright,
Whispered secrets by starlit night.
Planets bickered, each one a fool,
And made bets on who's next to drool!

Fragments of a Celestial Story

A bit of stardust, a twist of fate,
Found a lost moon on a long dinner date.
The sun made jokes that made it shine,
While the cosmos giggled over sips of brine.

Saturn's rings were made of pasta,
Dancing with Neptune, the space marasta.
Galaxies traded their very last pairs,
And told wild tales, full of spacey glares!

The Moment Between

In the blink of a star, all went awry,
A raccoon in space reached for the sky.
It slipped on a comet, oh what a sight,
As laughter erupted into the night.

An owl with glasses cheered with glee,
"Who knew the cosmos could be so free?"
For in every shadow, in every beam,
Lurks a moment that makes you beam!

Visions of the Unseen

In shadows cast by a giant thumb,
A raccoon thinks he's found a crumb.
The moon's wearing shades, what a sight!
As stars giggle, igniting the night.

A cat with a cape dances on air,
Demanding attention with effortless flair.
The planets have brunch, how absurd!
As comets deliver their best bird.

Jupiter jokes about the great Mars,
While Saturn spins tales of odd memoirs.
The cosmos is one big circus show,
With laughter that makes the stardust glow.

Tales of the Celestial Divide

Up in the sky, there's a wacky parade,
Where aliens compete in a cosmic charade.
The sun, with a wink, throws confetti so bright,
While the clouds wear hats, oh what a sight!

A rabbit hops by with a space helmet on,
Claiming he's searching for the great dawn.
The stars burst out laughing, what a riot!
Calling out, 'Hey, where's the quiet?'

The Milky Way's milkshake spills all around,
As meteors crash without making a sound.
Giggles resound through the deep dark expanse,
While cosmic jokers invent a new dance.

Reflections of the Forgotten Light

When a lone star shimmies by,
And trips on a moonbeam, oh my!
The darkness rolls over in fits of delight,
Creating a show that lasts through the night.

A squirrel on Mars tells tales with a grin,
About chasing a nebula and almost winning.
While Pluto, in jest, claims he's a king,
Wearing a crown made of cosmic bling.

The glow of the night plays tricks on the wise,
As comets slip by with a stolen surprise.
In the dance of the shadows, laughter takes flight,
The forgotten light brings joy to the night.

In the Embrace of Dusk

When dusk embraces the sky's gentle hue,
Even the crickets tap in a crew.
They sing to the stars a silly old tune,
As fireflies spark like the bright afternoon.

A donut-shaped galaxy spins with a joke,
While the asteroids dance in a frosty cloak.
"Do you believe in life on a cake?"
They giggle and shimmer on that cosmic break.

The evening holds secrets wrapped up in fun,
As light-hearted banter is swiftly begun.
With each twinkling dot laughing through dusk,
Life's silly moments spark joy like a musk.

Dreams in the Dark

When shadows dance and giggle light,
A cat in pajamas takes to flight.
The moon starts tickling the stars up high,
They laugh together, oh me, oh my!

A sandwich floats past on a cosmic breeze,
It slapped a planet with plenty of cheese.
Dreams take a stroll in the velvet night,
Chasing their tails in a twinkling fright.

Light's Lament

A beam of light slips on a banana peel,
It lands in a puddle, oh what a reel!
The sun wears sunglasses, feeling quite cool,
While shadows play tag, breaking all rules.

The glow bugs gathered for a bright parade,
But one climbed a lamp and became quite dismayed.
"What's the point of shining?" one bug did ask,
When being so bright is a difficult task!"

Cosmic Journeys

A comet rode in on a rainbow flare,
With roller skates on, it twirled in the air.
Stars cheered and clapped with glittery hands,
As they traveled through space, all bursting like bands.

They stumbled on Earth, in a silly race,
With aliens giggling, making a mess of space.
"Let's break out the snacks!" one star did decree,
As they munched on some stardust giggling with glee.

The Veil of Night

The night wore a cape, all dotted with stars,
A raccoon in shades was driving a car.
It zipped through the sky, to everyone's glee,
"Watch out for that meteor!" shouted a bee.

The owls held a dance, with tops and a hat,
They wobbled and spun to the tunes of a cat.
The night chuckled softly at all of the fun,
With dreams all aglow, until rise of the sun.

Shimmering Dreams of Darkness

When the moon wore a silly grin,
The sun decided to take a spin.
Stars giggled in their fancy attire,
While the night whispered, 'What a fire!'

A cat jumped high, chasing light,
It thudded down, what a sight!
The world beneath, in a lazy trance,
While shadows danced in a cosmic romance.

Wishes flew on a comet's tail,
Each one wobbled, some turned pale.
What happens when day gets shy?
Oh, the silliness that fills the sky!

A toast to all the creatures above,
Rabbits, raccoons, even a dove.
Let's laugh when the dark takes the floor,
And turn our frowns to cosmic lore!

The Great Convergence

Once the moon tried to steal the show,
The sun said, 'No way, I'll glow!'
Planets chuckled from afar,
'Who needs a spotlight? We're bizarre!'

Twirling twists in a celestial game,
A dance-off ensued, how insane!
Saturn wore rings, a flashy display,
While Venus tripped—what a ballet!

Asteroids joined in the fun parade,
With comets making a grand charade.
Milky Way laughed till it cried,
At the cosmic circus, jokes applied!

In the midst of this heavenly fuss,
Stars shouted, 'We're all one of us!'
So join the riot, let out a cheer,
It's a party up there—so sincere!

Fables Wreathed in Umbra

Once a snail with a shell so bright,
Thought he'd glide through the dark of night.
But bumping into a shadowy wall,
Cried, 'Is this my last waltz and call?'

A wise old owl hooted with glee,
"It's just a cloak for you to see.
Nothing's lost on this veiled dance,
Just waltz it off, take a chance!"

The shadows giggled, dashed around,
While critters cheered—what a sound!
In the dark, tales took a spin,
Each creature wore a grin from chin to chin.

So toast to shadows, the whimsical sort,
Crafting tales in their nightly court.
With laughter as bright as the morning beam,
Come join the fun in this delightful dream!

The Constellation's Secret

A goldfish said, 'I'm the star tonight!'
While a bird squawked, 'That isn't right!'
The constellations whispered and chuckled,
As the moonlit giggles suddenly huddled.

'They're just playing,' the comet winked,
'Watch the sky, see how it blinked!'
Stars put on sunglasses, looked quite grand,
Spinning tricks in a celestial band.

The clouds rolled in, wearing shades of gray,
'Time for a change-up! Let's play!'
With giggles galore, they bowed and swayed,
Throwing a concert—best plans displayed.

In a cosmic twist of funny fate,
All joined in to celebrate.
So here's a secret—whispered bright,
Every star loves a good laugh at night!

The Veiled Passage

In shadows, we dance and play,
A giant cheese wheel on display.
With hands in the air, we sway,
A cosmic game of hide and fray.

Lunacy spins, the stars now tease,
As comets sneeze and who knows, wheeze!
We giggle at the sky's grand tease,
While eating popcorn with such ease.

Uniformity and Chaos

In order, the planets march in line,
But one tripped over a cosmic vine.
While gravity pulls, they twist and twine,
Creating a show that's quite divine.

The sun winks down, "Leave me alone!"
As meteors complain, "We want a throne!"
Stars wearing hats, oh what a tone,
In this raucous, celestial zone.

Enigma of the Night Sky

The moon wears shades, it's a sunny plight,
While stars engage in friendly fights.
Constellations giggle, what a sight,
As they write love notes in pure starlight.

Twinkling lights break out in song,
While a telescope yells, "What could be wrong?
A wild meteor rushes along,
Crafting a tale that's terribly long."

The Great Covering

A blanket of darkness, snug and tight,
While shadows dance with pure delight.
"Hide and seek!" the stars shout in fright,
As they hide behind the sun's bright light.

With a sense of humor in the void,
The cosmos jests, never paranoid.
Silly antics, nothing is toyed,
In this grand show, we're all overjoyed.

Reflections in a Solar Veil

In a box, a shadow danced,
Chasing rays, it took a chance.
A squirrel squawked in sunlit glee,
"Is that a moon or just my tea?"

A lightbulb flickered, lost its way,
Disguised as night, it went to play.
Neighbors peeked, all filled with dread,
"What's going on? Did someone lose their head?"

The dog wore shades, looking divine,
Ignoring the cats who thought it a sign.
But every time the sky turned gray,
The ice cream truck would come out to play!

So when it glows, just grab your fluff,
Life's a party, that's enough!
The sun will shine, the moon will play,
We'll dance until the break of day.

Odes to the Inverted Sky

A crow on stilts, oh what a sight,
Flips and flops with pure delight.
The stars held hands, on velvet drapes,
And laughed aloud at silly shapes.

Oh how the clouds began to churn,
With fluffy jokes they took a turn.
A thunderclap, a giggle, a grin,
"Is that my sandwich? Oh, let's dive in!"

When rainbows sprout like wild confetti,
The world turns topsy in a jetty.
With jellyfish hosting a grand parade,
And dolphins wearing glasses, all homemade!

So, dear friends, tip your hat wide,
Join the circus, take a ride!
For dawn and dusk are just a jest,
In this upside-down, wacky fest.

The Midnight Saga

A cat in boots began to sing,
While owls threw a midnight fling.
With biscuits stacked like towers tall,
They held a party—come one, come all!

A shadow passed, then wore a mustache,
Stirring up trouble in a mad dash.
"Is that a comet or just my hat?
Let's find out—maybe it's just a cat!"

The tick-tock clock began to groan,
While fireflies flashed, their dance intone.
"More cookies, please!" the raccoons cried,
As tiny ghosts joined the raucous ride.

With marshmallows floating in the night,
It seems that dreams took wondrous flight.
Oh, what a tale, so much to share,
In the midnight hour, laughter fills the air!

Phantoms of the Luminescent Void

A ghost on roller skates swirled by,
Exclaiming loudly, "Watch me fly!"
Balloons were popping, making sounds,
As ghouls played jump rope, bouncing bounds.

The echoes giggled, shadows pranced,
While barking bats formed a weird dance.
"Who turned the lights off? Oh, my stars!
I think we're lost, in dance, on Mars!"

The moon was made of cheddar cheese,
And mice held feasts beneath the trees.
A pirate ship sailed through the mist,
With candy treasure, too good to resist!

So, if you wander in this strange night,
Prepare for treats, and pure delight!
For in the void, with laughter so bold,
The unexpected tales of life unfold.

The Crescendo of Twilight

As the sun plays peek-a-boo,
The shadows all start to swoon.
A chicken in a cape flies by,
Yelling, "Watch out for the moon!"

The dog dons glasses, quite the sight,
Chasing squirrels with all his might.
The picnic table starts to dance,
As ants prepare their daring prance.

In the sky, a comet winks,
While your cat's plotting food and drinks.
The crickets in tuxedos sing,
As stars join in, their twinkling bling.

And as the dusk gives way to play,
We join the wild and funny fray.
So grab a snack and take a seat,
This party's full of silly heat!

Secrets in the Gloom

In the corner where shadows creep,
Lies a goblin, fast asleep.
With a snore that could wake the dead,
He dreams of pies stacked up in red.

A bat in glasses, reading news,
Chuckles at the silly clues.
While owls argue who's the best,
In a debate that feels like jest.

Ghosts tell tales of pizza nights,
Comparing who can fly the highest.
With giggles echoing through the night,
The gloom is filled with pure delight.

And as the moon pulls out a chair,
A party forms without a care.
So when the night takes center stage,
Expect a laugh on every page!

Luminary's Last Stand

When heroes fail, they bite the dust,
In capes that flop, and masks of rust.
A superhero once lost his cape,
Tripped on a cat, fell through a scrape.

Fumbling gadgets, oops! How clumsy,
He makes the villains feel quite funny.
The sidekick sneezed, and with a boom,
The villain slipped in a burst of gloom.

As lights flicker in a quirky dance,
The crowd roars loud, they take the chance.
With laughter echoing through the land,
Defenders claim a victory grand!

Yet in the chaos, snacks appear,
Popcorn flies through the atmosphere.
Who needs to fight? Let's just unwind,
With fun, it seems, they're not far behind!

Fables of the Fading Light

Once upon a time in twilight's glow,
A fox read tales from long ago.
With every page, a laugh would ring,
As trees would dance and fairies sing.

A turtle claimed he'd run a race,
While bunnies bounced with silly grace.
The moon snickered, a keen observer,
As storytime found its fervor.

But wait, what's this? A wobbly chair,
Declaring war on the evening air.
With laughter loud, the night grew bright,
In fables spun, they took to flight!

So gather 'round and lend an ear,
For tales of fun that bring us cheer.
In dusk's embrace, we laugh and scheme,
In twilight's glow, we live the dream!

Threads of Light and Shade

In the sky, the moon wears a hat,
Sun gives a frown, oh imagine that!
Stars giggle while they play peek-a-boo,
Who knew night could wear such a shoe?

Planets dance a wobbly jig,
Comets chase, it's a cosmic dig.
A solar game of hide and seek,
Pulling pranks, they're all unique!

Daytime's bold, but night's a tease,
Whispering jokes on a cosmic breeze.
Light slips and slides through the sky's veil,
Even the sun begins to pale!

So grab your glasses, sit right tight,
Watch the show of dark and light.
With laughter echoing through the night,
The universe puts on quite a sight!

Melodies of the Transient

A raucous jam in the cosmic hall,
Stars strumming chords that seem to call.
Moonlight sings a ballad so bright,
While shadows dance far out of sight.

The sun plays drums, a lively beat,
While planets chirp, oh what a feat!
Galaxies twirl in a dizzy spree,
Creating laughter, oh, can't you see?

In this catchy tune of the vast unknown,
Where shadows wink and giggles are grown.
Every twinkling star adds a note,
To the melody that floats like a boat.

So join the fun, clap your hands,
In this orchestra of bizarre bands.
The harmony of light and shade,
Leaves us grinning, blissfully played!

Echoes of the Hidden Realm

In the distance, a chuckle takes flight,
From comets zooming past so light.
Whispers from stars, soft as a breeze,
Echoing secrets through cosmic trees.

The sun winks, a cheeky spark,
While the moon spins tales in the dark.
Planets giggle at the moon's prance,
In this wacky, celestial dance!

Galactic jokes, twisted and round,
Make even the asteroids bounce off the ground.
Hiding behind clouds, the stars take a peek,
When the night falls, the fun's at its peak.

So listen close to the starlit cheer,
As laughter rings through the atmosphere.
These echoes of light, a silly repeal,
In the realm of shadows, oh, what a steal!

The Great Umbra

A curious show at the world's edge,
Where the shadow meets the sun's pledge.
In the spotlight, a playful scene,
With cosmic creatures clad in sheen.

The moon tiptoes, a sneaky tease,
While the sun grumbles, "Oh, if you please!"
Their comedic rivalry sure brings a laugh,
As shadows flare in a silly gaffe.

From dusk till dawn, the antics unfold,
With stories more ridiculous than gold.
A hide-and-seek with light so jolly,
Belly laughs bounce through this cosmic folly.

So let's applaud this grand display,
Where laughter twinkles night and day.
The great shadow ballet spins and twirls,
In this universe of giggles and swirls!

Radiance and Ruin

A bright sun played hide and seek,
While the moon snickered, so to speak.
They juggled shadows with a wink,
While the stars giggled, on the brink.

The earth just shrugged, said, 'What the fuss?'
As the cat complained, 'I'm missing my bus!'
The world spun on, with cosmic cheer,
While a dog barked loud, 'I'm stuck right here!'

The sun scolded, 'Now, don't be rude!'
The moon replied, 'I'm just in the mood.'
The galaxy spun in a goofy dance,
As comets wiggled, giving a chance.

Yet, in the chaos, there's laughter bright,
A cosmic joke in the midst of night.
Stars rolled their eyes, with a sparkle and gleam,
As the universe giggled, or so it would seem.

Shadows Over Ancient Lands

Once golden rays brought stories bold,
Now there's a shadow, if truth be told.
Old pyramids scratched their weary heads,
Wondering where the sunlight bled.

A pharaoh sighed, 'What's with this shade?'
While mummies danced, saying, 'We weren't made!'
Camel humps bobbed in a silly beat,
As sand dunes chuckled, losing their seat.

Time travelers stopped, to take a look,
At shadowy creatures reading a book.
'What's happening here?' they scratched their chin,
'I'd say it's a plot twist, where to begin?'

The ruins grinned at the blatant fun,
'Even shadows need light, let's run!'
And so they raced, with a gleeful shout,
As shadows danced, dispelling their doubt.

The Darkened Horizon

A horizon stretched, darkened and wide,
With whispers of laughter the stars can't hide.
The sun said, 'Don't leave me in gloom!'
While the moon just giggled, 'Give me more room!'

Clouds frolicked past with a mischievous grin,
'We're just here to add a little spin.'
While the wind snickered, tugging at trees,
'Come join the party, topples with ease!'

A pirate ship sailed through the twilight,
Claiming the skies, oh what a sight!
They'll steal the stars, or so they swore,
But tripped on shadows, fell over the floor.

It's a ruckus, where darkness reigns,
Yet laughter echoes through solar chains.
So here's to the dusk, where all is bright,
In the chaos of night, there's cosmic delight!

Celestial Legends Unfold

Under starlit tales of yore,
Legends were born, and laughter swore.
The constellations, in silly disguise,
Created a story, to everyone's surprise.

Orion tripped, and fell on his bow,
While Cassiopeia shouted, 'This isn't allowed!'
A star exploded in comedic flair,
As comets chuckled, swirling in air.

The Milky Way quipped, 'Is this a jest?'
While planets filled in for a cosmic fest.
'Just bend the rules, and join in the fun!'
As stardust sprinkled, for everyone.

So gather 'round, for stories soar,
With laughter echoing forevermore.
In this universe, with joy so bold,
Celestial legends delightfully unfold.

Shifting Celestial Tales

A giant cheese wheel rolls on high,
The moon sneezes with a goofy sigh.
Stars chuckle as they twirl around,
While planets giggle, joy unbound.

The sun is winking, what a tease,
Jupiter's dancing with such ease.
Comets zoom in silly flights,
While aliens play silly pranks at night.

The cosmos laughs, a joy parade,
Galaxies are in a masquerade.
A meteor sings a funny tune,
While Saturn twirls with a spoon.

In this vast and merry spree,
Gravity trips, oh can't you see?
Referencing tales of old, quite bold,
As laughter sparkles like stars of gold.

Shadowed Journeys

In shadows cast by laughter's glow,
The moon's a joker, stealing the show.
Stars stick out their silly tongues,
While cosmic giggles rhyme like songs.

Planets bop in a jovial dance,
While meteors take a chance to prance.
A black hole yawns with a chuckle sly,
As cosmic winds tease breezes nigh.

The comets wear their party hats,
Zipping by like playful cats.
In this journey of the kooky sky,
Even the sun admits it's shy.

Asteroids joke but miss the mark,
As stardust twirls dance with a spark.
In night's embrace, we find our cheer,
For the mundane's taken a backseat here!

Celestial Reverie

Caught in whims of starry jest,
The moon's a clown, it likes to pest.
Shooting stars wear giant shoes,
Wobbling under cosmic blues.

All the planets laugh and tease,
While Saturn spins with unexpected ease.
Even the sun throws in a wink,
As comet tails go 'pop!' and link.

Twinkling dreams with giggles bright,
Galaxies grinning in delight.
Asteroids chuckle and roll about,
In this reverie, there's no doubt.

In this far-off place of fun and glee,
Stardust holds a carnival spree.
Join the chorus of playful skies,
Even the echoes join in, oh my!

Whispers of the Darkened Sky

When night falls down with a joyful sigh,
Stars play hide-and-seek, oh my!
The moon whispers secrets to a comet fast,
"Don't trip on the tail, you'll fall at last!"

Darkness giggles, a mischievous friend,
Twirling shadows, merry to lend.
The sun peeks in with a grin so wide,
As starry faces can't help but bide.

In this tapestry of laughs that fly,
The universe winks and won't say why.
Through the night, whimsical tales unfold,
Of cosmic jesters, brave and bold.

Each flicker ignites a joyous spark,
Under the canopy, with a cheeky remark.
So let's dance and spin till dawn's bright door,
For laughter echoes forevermore.

The Luminous Abyss

In the dark, a fun parade,
Moon in shades, a playful charade.
Stars do giggle, stretch and bend,
Earthbound folks just wave and send.

When shadows slide like sneaky cats,
Laughing lights wear funny hats.
Dancing suns, all in good cheer,
How they play and disappear!

Winking comets whistle tunes,
Playful banter with the moons.
Solar rays on a frolic spree,
Plotting mischief, wild and free.

A cosmic joke, with punchlines bright,
In this swirling, silly night.
Watch those orbs with giggles swell,
In the void, all's well, do tell!

Journeys Through the Celestial Canvas

On the canvas of night, a splash,
Stars waltz by, a friendly crash.
Brush strokes whirl, colors collide,
Galaxies boast, they're quite the ride.

Jupiter bounces, skips with glee,
While Venus teases, 'Come dance with me!'
Checkered skies, with clouds in tow,
Tickling suns put on a show.

Shooting stars play peek-a-boo,
'Catch me quick!' they gleefully woo.
With every twist, a pun unfurls,
In the canvas, joy swirls and twirls.

Join the fun, don't miss the spree,
Galactic giggles await, you'll see.
In this realm where laughter's king,
Paint your dreams, let your heart sing!

Dances of the Shaded Cosmos

In the shadows, a party of hues,
Moonlight jiggles in sparkly shoes.
Stars prance round, in dizzy delight,
While comets crash, oh what a sight!

Nebulas twist in dramatic flair,
A cosmic dance, beyond compare.
Galaxies whirl, a tango so grand,
Painting the void, hand in hand.

Saturn spins with its ringed attire,
While Mars plays tunes on a phony lyre.
Oh, what laughter fills the space,
As celestial bodies join the race!

So join the frolic, lose your woes,
In this stellar ball, anything goes!
With every twirl, hear the laughter's rise,
As the universe winks with bright eyes!

The Twilight Tapestry

In twilight threads, where colors blend,
The day winks back, with moments to send.
Silly clouds march, all in line,
While shadows stretch, oh how they twine!

Sunbeams play, a hide and seek,
Whispering secrets, oh so chic.
As the day takes its cozy bow,
Stars will twinkle, here and now.

Giggles echo where the sky meets the ground,
In this tapestry, joy is found.
With every stitch, a story spins,
Of clever whims and playful grins.

So laugh along with the fading light,
Dance in dreams, hold on tight!
For in this realm where mirth does thrive,
The tapestry of night comes alive!

New Moons and Old Tales

In shadows deep, the cats all play,
Chasing dogs who run away.
Goldfish swim in pots of jam,
While old folks dance like they're in a jam.

A turtle wears a captain's hat,
Dances with a dancing rat.
They sail the seas of silver soup,
Where spoons hold parties for the goop.

On merry nights, the stars will wink,
As pickle jars begin to think.
With tales of cheese and flying shoes,
Understanding all the silly blues.

So gather round, let laughter ring,
With every tasty, silly thing.
For when the night swallows the day,
Old tales laugh, come out to play.

The Hum of the Hidden Stars

In hidden realms, the glowbugs hum,
Invisible bands, oh what a drum!
They form a choir, just like the bears,
Who dance with style, while tickling their hairs.

The ants throw balls in silver shoes,
While frogs recite their best rhymes and blues.
Stars in skirts do a moonlit jig,
And snickersnacks bounce, oh so big!

A pencil's tip once made a wish,
To swim with dolphins in a dish.
Tickled pink, the night sky sighs,
While dreams float under noodle pies.

So if you see a glowing tail,
It's just the stars who love to sail.
In laughter's arms, they twist and twirl,
As night wraps all in a sparkly swirl.

Chronicles in the Gloaming

When shadows stretch their arms so wide,
The world giggles, no need to hide.
Toasters dance in twinkling lights,
While bold old socks start silly fights.

Crickets gather with their friends,
Telling tales that twist and bend.
With marshmallow clouds that giggle and sway,
While moonbeans bounce through the bakery's spray.

A clownfish wears a feathered neck,
Winks at seahorses, "What the heck?"
They paint the waves with brushy strokes,
And laugh aloud with silly jokes.

When gloaming comes, let fun begin,
For every silly grin's a win.
With stories spun in every glow,
The night invites a merry show.

Legends Carved in Night

In the midnight hour when cats recite,
Their grand old legends of the night.
With moose in coats and unicorn shoes,
They hold debates on what to choose.

Popcorn clouds drift in a dance,
As squirrels practice their weekly prance.
Octopuses juggle with spaghetti strands,
While bumblebees play in marching bands.

Each star a whisper, each twinkle a tale,
Of donkeys flying with wings on their sail.
They dream of giant cupcakes tossed,
Laughing about all the frosting lost.

So come and hear the stories bright,
Carved in the fabric of the night.
With every giggle and silly cheer,
Legends unfold, come gather here!

Shadowed Revelations

The moon stole the sun's bright hat,
A giggle echoed, 'What's up with that?'
Stars winked in their cosmic glee,
While the sun yelled, 'Hey, let me be!'

Cats in sunglasses raised a toast,
To the shadow that soon became a ghost.
The earth twirled in a silly dance,
Creating warmth in a playful trance.

Celestial Chronicles

Once upon a time, in night's embrace,
The moon slipped out for a silly chase.
Up above, the stars held a party,
And the sun got mad, said, 'This is too hearty!'

Planets juggled with comets in tow,
Spreading confetti, making a show.
Galaxies laughed at a quasar's joke,
As their cosmic balloons began to poke.

The Dance of Darkness

In twilight's skip, the shadows pranced,
Each star behind a curtain danced.
The moon wore a crown, made from cheese,
Swaying 'round like it aimed to please.

A solar spotlight flashed a grin,
Making the planets spin in a din.
They twirled and twinkled, a sight to see,
As comets joined in, wild and free.

Tales Beyond the Veil

In a void where light plays peek-a-boo,
Galactic myths, they grew and grew.
Starfishes traded stories of light,
While meteors zoomed, a comical sight.

Black holes told tales with gaping mouths,
Sucking in giggles, dispersing them south.
The universe chuckled, 'What a grand show!'
As laughter echoed, from high to low.

A Journey through the Obscured

In the dark, the sun began to pout,
Cheese sandwich forgot, or so it's about.
Sky's silly dance, clouds twirling in their feat,
As folks below scramble for a snack to eat.

Shadows play peekaboo, a game quite absurd,
A cat on a rooftop just quietly stirred.
All eyes are up, like goldfish in a bowl,
Cheering on rock stars, the moon takes a stroll.

With every flash of light, a story's unfurled,
Is that a star or my neighbor's old world?
Giggles erupt; laughter fills the air,
Truth takes a vacation—no one seems to care.

The antics of nature, a cosmic delight,
As we ponder our snacks in starry twilight.
With whimsy and wonder, the night feels alive,
A comical journey, where we all just thrive.

Stars Behind the Masks

Stars play dress-up, wearing wigs made of light,
Hiding from cameras, avoiding the fright.
Do they have secrets? Perhaps a wild dance,
Twinkling at us, with a flirty glance.

The moon's wearing shades, such a funky sight,
Paired with a comet, oh what a delight!
Together they giggle, in the dark they prance,
Grinning like kids, making mischief enhance.

Galaxies gossip, over drinks made of stardust,
Chatting away while we all sit in trust.
Under this canopy, laughter takes flight,
As constellations wink, gleaming so bright.

Laughter erupts as meteors race,
Sprinkling the night with their shimmering grace.
Our hearts keep on soaring; oh, what a dream,
In this cosmic arena, we all laugh and beam.

Chasing Dimming Horizons

Running after shadows, we sprint and we slide,
With golden-hued giggles, we let hope be our guide.
The sun winks back, playing hide and seek,
As we leap into colors, each moment unique.

A parade of moments, swirling and bright,
Like ice cream cones melting on a warm summer night.
We dance as the lights flicker, oh what a sight,
Chasing the dimming, with spirits so light.

Oh, the sky is a canvas, it changes with flair,
We paint it with laughter, and joy fills the air.
The horizon's our playground, with wishes we scribble,
Chasing the dimming, we laugh and we giggle.

With each fading glimmer, a cheer lifts us high,
As we toast to the stars with a slice of the pie.
And though daylight may beckon, we'll carry the night,
In our hearts, the echoes of laughter take flight.

Luminous Legends

Once upon a starball, legends did roam,
Talking turtles dressed in glitter, made their home.
They spun great tall tales of cosmic delight,
While the comets formed bands, jamming all night.

With melodies silly, they struck a great chord,
The moon grooved along, playing soft turquoise chord.
Shooting stars twerked, surprise on their face,
As we listened in awe, in this magical space.

The sun's laughter echoed, a bright golden tune,
While midnight goblins planned a birthday balloon.
With each astronomic tale, laughter cascades,
Creating a bonanza of luminous charades.

We strolled with the fluff of fantastical dreams,
In a night full of giggles and starlit beams.
Thus legends they tell, with humor on stage,
As we dance through the cosmos, bold and all sage.

Nightfall Narratives

When shadows crawl and dance with glee,
A cat's on guard, sipping herbal tea.
The moon is teasing, donning a grin,
While stars play chess, letting the games begin.

The sun is snoozing, wrapped in a sheet,
While crickets chirp a catchy beat.
A squirrel on stilts, what a bizarre sight,
As laughter bubbles up through the night.

The owls are hooting a feathery tune,
While rabbits hop, beneath a balloon.
The night has stories, both silly and bright,
Sharing secrets of folly 'til morning's first light.

So here's to the night, with joy we embrace,
A world full of whimsy, just set the pace.
With giggles and grins till the dawn's early ray,
Let's dance with the shadows, come join the play!

Battlegrounds of Light

Two armies clash in a cosmic ballet,
With beams of laughter leading the fray.
A sunbeam tickles the moon's silvery cheek,
While planets throw pies, oh what a week!

Mars redirects, with a grandiose plan,
In his helmet of cheese, how absurd for a man!
Jupiter juggles while Saturn spins news,
In the epic showdown of leafy green hues.

The stars are the spectators, sipping sweet tea,
As meteors zoom, in a sparkly spree.
With each zany move, mischief ignites,
In the light's lively dance, the laughter ignites.

So gather your wits, let the absurd take flight,
In this hilarious brawl between day and night.
With fireworks popping in a sky painted high,
We cheer for the fun, as we laugh and fly!

The Unseen Passage

In a twisty tunnel of glimmer and haze,
Strange creatures wander in a daze.
A fox in a cape does the Macarena dance,
While shadows do the tango, given a chance.

The flicker of lights, like fireflies play,
Nudging the moon to join in the fray.
A pair of old socks start a spirited race,
Through the unseen passage, a chaotic place.

A time-traveling fish swims up to the sky,
With dreams of a vacation, oh me, oh my!
Starlight sings softly to sleepy old trees,
As giggles collide in a playful breeze.

Let's stroll through this space where the wacky abound,
In the unseen passage, laughter's unbound.
With echoes of joy lighting the way,
We dance with the shadows till the break of day!

Chronicles of the Delta Dawn

When the first light spills over the hill,
The frogs put on top hats, what a thrill!
A rooster crows in a curious key,
While squirrels conduct a symphony spree.

The river giggles as it splishes and splashes,
With ducks that wear shades and make quirky dashes.
Sunflowers giggle in their bright, golden gowns,
As dawn paints the sky in whimsical crowns.

A parade of insects marches in line,
Carrying sugar and tea, oh so fine!
With ants on a mission for honey and jam,
In the chronicles of dawn, we all say, "Ma'am!"

So raise up your cups to the day's funny wake,
Let's dance with the critters and laugh for their sake.
As the sun stretches wide with a warm, silly cheer,
In the chronicles of dawn, joy is all near!

When Light Defies the Night

A moonbeam dance with a wink,
The sun told night, 'Take a drink!'
Stars giggled, their shine on parade,
While shadows plotted, unafraid.

A solar chuckle, a lunar jest,
Who knew the dark could be such a pest?
As daylight peeks and twilight spills,
Everyone laughs, ignoring the chills.

The night wore pajamas, quite out of style,
While dawn tickled it, with a bright smile.
Mirth echoed through the cosmic swirl,
Who knew the universe had such a whirl?

When light plays pranks, oh what a sight,
The sun and moon throw a playful fight.
In the sky, a concert of glee,
Where nighttime's secrets become a spree.

Cosmic Shrouds

A blanket of stars with clumsy seams,
Wraps the cosmos in wobbly beams.
Planets tossed like salad greens,
Float in the void, making strange scenes.

A comet sneezes, brings in a breeze,
While galaxies spin, as they please.
Supernova farts, causing a ruckus,
The universe giggles, oh what a circus!

Asteroids dodge like they're playing tag,
While black holes burp, saying 'How's that?'
The Milky Way winks with a saucy grin,
In this chaos, it's all a win!

Between the planets, laughter erupts,
As starlight jumps in its playful ducts.
The cosmic cloth, a tapestry wild,
Holds stories of stars, all dancing like a child.

The Temporal Odyssey

Time's a jester with a floppy hat,
Turning minutes into a chat!
Hours spill like jellybeans,
While seconds race on speedy machines.

Mismatched clocks on a silly quest,
Tick-tock laughter, feeling blessed.
Time travelers trip, and fumble too,
They're stuck at lunch, with nowhere to chew.

Past and future in a pie fight,
Messy timelines brought to light.
Present day, with cake on its face,
Laughing hard, keeping up the pace.

Each tick a giggle, each tock a cheer,
In the realm of time, nothing to fear!
With dances and pranks across the span,
A joyful journey, that's the plan!

Whispers in the Twilight

As day drips down, with a blush so sweet,
The night peeks out, ready to compete.
Fireflies flicker, telling secrets too,
While the moon wears shades, feeling cool and new.

Twilight's giggles, soft and clear,
Bubble up like a fizzy beer.
Cats in the alley, plotting their schemes,
Waiting to pounce, just like in dreams.

A breeze tickles trees, with gentle finesse,
As shadows creep in, no time to rest.
The sky swirls pink, purple, and blue,
While crickets sing their evening cue.

In this moment, all feel alive,
As stars play hide-and-seek, they thrive.
With whispers of laughter, the night unfurls,
A tapestry woven, in a swirl of pearls.

In the Eye of the Night

The moon wore shades, quite bold and bright,
To strut its stuff in the middle of the night.
Stars were gossiping, oh what a sight,
While comets danced in gallant flight.

A cat complained beneath the glow,
"Can't a guy just take it slow?"
The owls hooted, a comical show,
As shadows pranced like a cabaret pro.

A flash of light, a meteor's race,
Made craters of laughter on the dull space.
If space is a stage, we're in the wrong place,
With popcorn ready, for this crazy chase.

In the eye of the night, they waltz and peek,
With twinkling eyes and a touch of cheek.
The night giggles with a playful shriek,
As the universe dances, just to bespeak.

Parables of Shadowed Time

In daylight's bustle, shadows do hide,
With tales of silliness, they bide their pride.
One whispered secrets, "Let's take a ride!"
Then tripped on a branch, oh what a slide!

The sun was joking, its rays on the lay,
"Who turned off the light? Come out and play!"
While clocks ticked loudly, just to dismay,
The shadows conspired to lead us astray.

A rake in the garden smirked at the fun,
As trowels and shovels were on the run.
"We're tools of the trade! Can we join, just one?"
They piled in a truck, oh what a bun!

At dusk, they toasted with mugs of cheer,
Revealed all the laughter they held so dear.
In the parables sung, we all draw near,
For mischief and joy keep the heart sincere.

An Odyssey in Twilight

A ship of shadows set sail at dusk,
With a crew of giggles, a humorous husk.
The captain sneezed, what a funny brusque,
As moondust twinkled, like world-class musk.

Stars gathered 'round for a jesting quest,
To find the horizon where laughs were best.
They sailed past comets in a feathered vest,
With jellybeans flying, they felt so blessed.

The mermaids giggled, having a ball,
With scales of laughter, their charms did enthrall.
"Why's the ocean blue? Tell us, or stall!"
"Because your jokes made the waves rise tall!"

As twilight descended, the crew started a dance,
With lanterns lit, each held a chance.
A night of fun, a cosmic romance,
In the odyssey of joy, they took their stance.

The Cosmic Veil

Behind a curtain of sparkling fun,
Giggled the galaxies, one by one.
The nebulae twinkled, all came undone,
In the cosmic whimsy of laughter spun.

Stars poked their heads from the fabric of night,
Saying, "Hey, earthlings! Come join our flight!"
With comets as ships, oh what a delight,
They laughed through the void, a cosmic invite.

The vacuum chuckled, a thumping bass beat,
As gravity danced with two left feet.
"Light travels fast but laughter's a treat,
Time slows for joy; let's share this feat!"

So here we go, on this astronomical ride,
With jokes that eclipse the mundane tide.
In the cosmic veil, let's laugh, let's glide,
For in humor's embrace, we can all reside.

Portals to the Unseen

In the midnight hour, cats wear capes,
Chasing shadows, making japes.
Monkeys dance on lunar beams,
Swinging high in moonlit dreams.

Sneaky squirrels in striped pajamas,
Stealing cookies, oh the dramas!
Whispers float on candy air,
As clowns in orbit start to stare.

The sun's a joker, taking a dip,
While wacky wishes take a trip.
Bananas fly with funny glee,
In our secret jubilee.

So grab your hats and hop on board,
Join the fest of the absurd.
For once the world spins askew,
The wildest dreams come rushing through.

Echoes of the Eclipse

When the sun wore a silly hat,
And stars played hide-and-seek with the cat.
Llamas sang in a shimmering groove,
As sleepy turtles began to move.

Clouds pulled pranks, oh what a sight,
Painting rainbows in the night.
Pandas crashed the cosmic show,
Rolling in stardust, just for show.

The moon juggled comets with flair,
While raccoons twirled in the air.
A chorus of giggles echoed wide,
As shadows danced and secrets cried.

In this realm where odd meets cheer,
We wave to time, oh bring it here!
For laughter's light, it shines so bright,
In this zany, endless night.

Veils of Time

Time wears a cloak stitched with jokes,
Giggling softly, playing with folks.
A turtle speeds past with a sigh,
Chasing a rabbit who walks on high.

Dancing clocks with silly hands,
Twist and twirl on time's demands.
The past wears shoes three sizes too small,
While future dreams bounce off the wall.

A quirky breeze whispers sweet tunes,
As kangaroos moonwalk among the dunes.
Pandoras dance in polka-dot shoes,
Poking fun at old tomorrows' blues.

Let's all step lightly with a grin,
As the landscapes twist and spin.
In this laughter-laden crime,
We embrace the veils of time!

Dusk's Silent Serenade

At dusk, the fireflies sing a song,
While owls hoot, don't get me wrong!
Goblins skateboard on beams of light,
Chasing dreams until it's night.

As shadows crawled with ticklish tricks,
The stars all laughed, what a mix!
Dancing mushrooms in a soft glow,
Wiggle and giggle, steal the show.

The moon whispers secrets quite absurd,
To the earth where laughter's heard.
Jellybeans tumble from the sky,
Making wishes as they fly.

So gather round for dusk's delight,
With silly songs and bubbly fright.
In this serenade, pure and bright,
We find the joy in the silent night.

Chronicles Beneath the Moon

There once was a moon quite round,
It giggled and wobbled when it found.
A sandwich of cheese, it swore,
Brought laughter on every shore.

The stars had a party in the sky,
But tripped on the clouds as they'd fly.
With disco balls and bright bling,
They jived to a celestial swing.

A comet zoomed by, quite unaware,
It messed up the hair of a bear.
The critter just rolled on the grass,
As meteors fell, oh what a class!

With shadows that danced on the ground,
The whispers of secrets profound.
Yet every so often they'd squeal,
In ticks of time, laughter they'd steal.

The Dance of Light and Shadow

In a realm where light meets the dark,
The shadow puppets made a spark.
With crazy moves and silly sights,
They turned dusk into delightful nights.

The sun said, "I'll take a break," with a grin,
While the moon brought in mischief to spin.
They played hide and seek, oh what a game,
Each claiming the other was to blame!

Balloons floated past in the breeze,
Making wishes on giggles with ease.
As constellations joined in the fun,
Their cosmic pranks had just begun.

Light tickled shadows, they burst into fits,
Creating a ruckus with cheerful bits.
Who knew that the night could be so fine,
With laughter echoing through space and time?

When Stars Align

When once in the sky stars aligned,
They formed silly shapes, oh so unrefined.
A toaster, a cat, and a sock on a chair,
In the great cosmic tale, they formed quite a pair.

The Milky Way giggled at their sight,
As they tossed popcorn, a real delight.
A meteor shower, a buttery rain,
With space critters dancing, oh what a gain!

Galactic jokes flew through the air,
Gravity lost in the cosmic fair.
"Why did the star not check the clock?"
"Because time is a prankster, it gave it a shock!"

So if you gaze up with a wink and a grin,
Remember the fun that began with a spin.
For when stars align, it's always a hoot,
In the cosmos where laughter takes root!

Tales from the Twilight Realm

In twilight's land where shadows grow,
A squirrel wore glasses, putting on a show.
With acorns as props, he danced with flair,
As owls hooted tunes that filled the air.

The hedgehogs rolled in a merry race,
Who'd clear the path, a comical chase.
The sun playfully dipped, then peeked,
Leaving chuckles and giggles, oh how they peaked!

Ghostly figures told tales from the night,
Of pumpkins that floated in floating flight.
"Once I was a king, in disguise as a beet,
Now I'm just laughing—can't take the heat!"

So if you wander 'neath stars that gleam,
Remember to chuckle, to smile and beam.
For in twilight's embrace, all pranks are the same,
The tales are a riot, never just plain!

www.ingramcontent.com/pod-product-compliance
Lightning Source LLC
Chambersburg PA
CBHW072140200426
43209CB00051B/185